Contents

Making a start

Learning to draw is about looking and seeing. Keep practising and get to know your subject. Use a sketchbook to make quick drawings. Start by doodling and experimenting with shapes and patterns. There are many ways to draw; this book shows only some methods. Visit art galleries, look at artists' drawings, see how friends draw, but above all, find your own way.

Use simple shapes to draw the figures in action.

Remember that practice makes perfect. If it
looks wrong, start again. Keep working at it —
the more you draw, the more you will learn.

5

Perspective

If you look at any object from different viewpoints, you will see that the part that is closest to you looks larger, and the part furthest away from you looks smaller. Drawing in perspective is a way of creating a feeling of space — of showing three dimensions on a flat surface.

V.P.

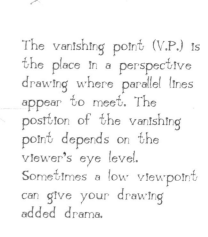

The vanishing point (V.P.) is the place in a perspective drawing where parallel lines appear to meet. The position of the vanishing point depends on the viewer's eye level. Sometimes a low viewpoint can give your drawing added drama.

6

Two-point perspective uses two
vanishing points: one for lines running
along the length of the object, and one
on the opposite side for lines running
across the width of the object.

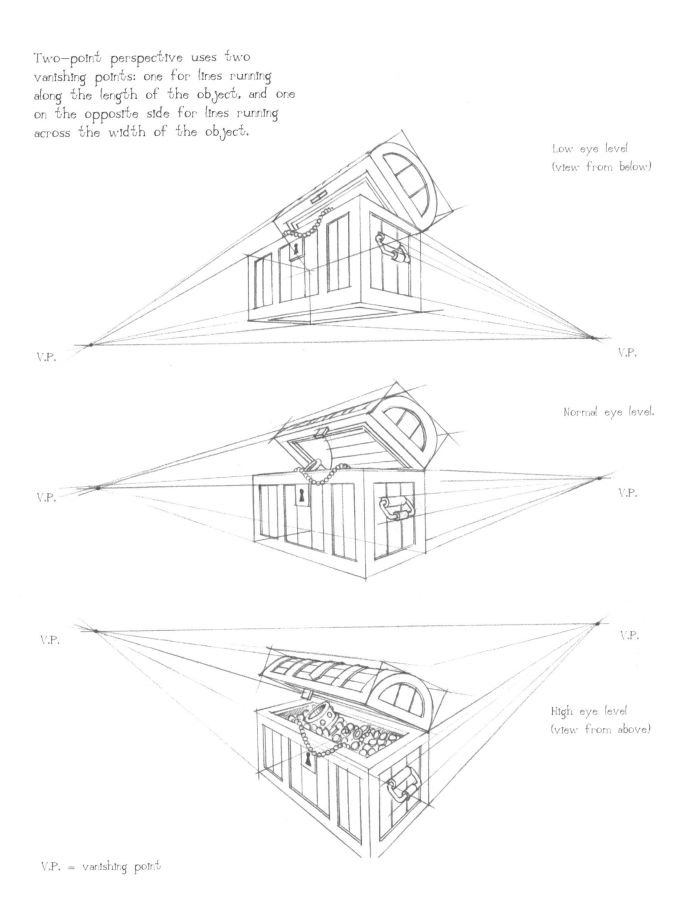

Low eye level
(view from below)

V.P.

V.P.

Normal eye level.

V.P.

V.P.

V.P.

V.P.

High eye level
(view from above)

V.P. = vanishing point

Drawing tools

Here are just a few of the many tools that you can use for drawing. Let your imagination go and have fun experimenting with all the different marks you can make.

Pencil

Watercolour pencil

Charcoal pencil

Charcoal stick

Pastels

Finger painting

Black, grey and white pastel on grey sugar paper

Each grade of **pencil** makes a different mark, from fine, grey lines through to soft, black ones. Hard pencils are graded as H, 2H, 3H, 4H, 5H and 6H (the hardest). An HB pencil is ideal for general sketching. Soft pencils are graded from B, 2B, 3B, 4B, 5B to 6B (the softest and blackest).

Watercolour pencils come in many different colours and make a line similar to an HB pencil. But paint over your finished drawing with clean water, and the lines will soften and run.

It is less messy and easier to achieve a fine line with a **charcoal pencil** than a stick of charcoal. Create soft tones by smudging lines with your finger. **Ask an adult** to spray the drawing with fixative to prevent further smudging.

Pastels are brittle sticks of powdered colour. They blend and smudge easily and are ideal for quick sketches. Pastel drawings work well on textured, coloured paper. **Ask an adult** to spray your finished drawing with fixative.

Experiment with **finger painting**. Your fingerprints make exciting patterns and textures. Use your fingers to smudge soft pencil, charcoal and pastel lines.

Ballpoint pens are very useful for sketching and making notes. Make different tones by building up layers of shading.

A **mapping pen** has to be dipped into bottled ink to fill the nib. Different nib shapes make different marks. Try putting a diluted ink wash over parts of the finished drawing.

Draughtsmen's pens and specialist **art pens** can produce extremely fine lines and are ideal for creating surface texture. A variety of pen nibs are available which produce different widths of line.

Felt—tip pens are ideal for quick sketches. If the ink is not waterproof, try drawing on wet paper and see what happens.

Broad—nibbed **marker pens** make interesting lines and are good for large, bold sketches. Try using a black pen for the main sketch and a grey one to block in areas of shadow.

Paintbrushes are shaped differently to make different marks. Japanese brushes are soft and produce beautiful flowing lines. Large sable brushes are good for painting a wash over a line drawing. Fine brushes are good for drawing delicate lines.

Ballpoint pen

Mapping pen

Draughtsman's pen

Felt—tip pen

Marker pen

Paintbrush

Materials

Try using different types of drawing paper and materials. Experiment with charcoal, wax crayons and pastels. All pens, from felt—tips to ballpoints, will make interesting marks — you could also try drawing with pen and ink on wet paper.

Felt—tips come in a range of line widths. The wider pens are good for filling in large areas of flat tone.

Silhouette is a style of drawing which mainly uses solid black shapes.

Ink silhouette

Hatching

Lines drawn in **ink** cannot be erased, so keep your ink drawings sketchy and less rigid. Don't worry about mistakes as these lines can be lost in the drawing as it develops.

Adding light and shade to a drawing with an ink pen can be tricky. Use a solid layer of ink for the very darkest areas and cross—hatching (straight lines criss—crossing each other) for ordinary dark tones. Hatching (straight lines running parallel to each other) can be used for midtones. Leave the lightest areas white.

Pencil drawings can include a vast amount of detail and tone. Try experimenting with different grades of pencil to get a range of light and shade effects in your drawing.

Remember the best equipment and materials will not necessarily make the best drawing — only practice will.

11

Pirate Hats

Pirates wear a variety of hats with different shapes and styles. Hats are best constructed along with the head so that they fit snugly together.

The style of a hat or headdress can make one character very different from another. On board ship, the style of hat can denote status.

Drawing a hat and head together helps you to understand how the hat fits around the head.

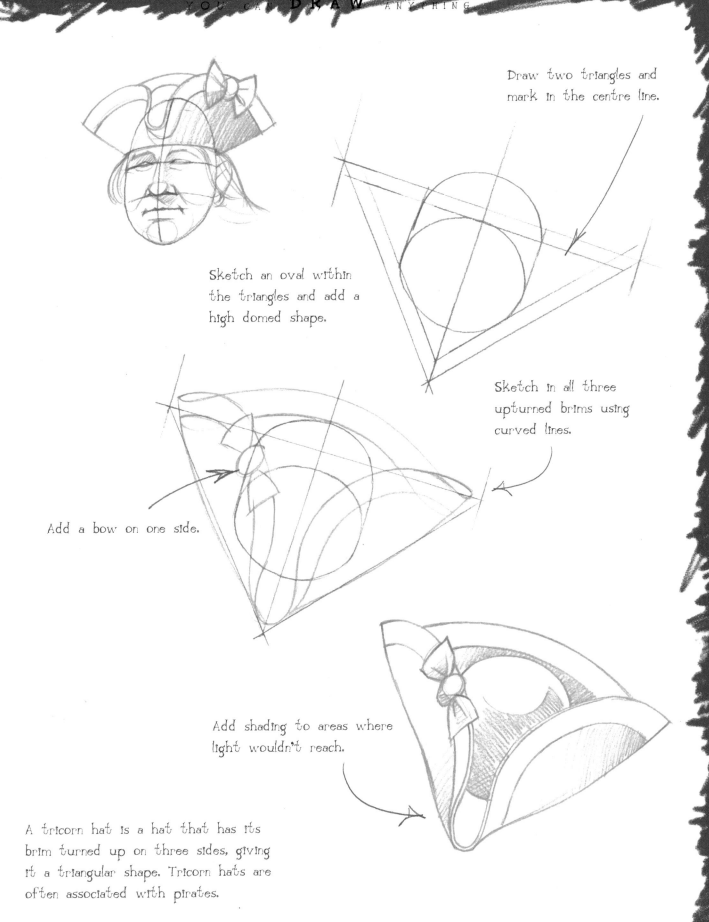

Draw two triangles and mark in the centre line.

Sketch an oval within the triangles and add a high domed shape.

Sketch in all three upturned brims using curved lines.

Add a bow on one side.

Add shading to areas where light wouldn't reach.

A tricorn hat is a hat that has its brim turned up on three sides, giving it a triangular shape. Tricorn hats are often associated with pirates.

Remove any unwanted construction lines.

13

Blackbeard

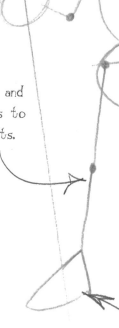

A fearsome pirate who terrorised all who sailed the Caribbean Seas. He carried six loaded pistols and famously tucked smouldering lit fuses under his hat so that the smoke would make him look even scarier.

Draw ovals for the head, body and hips.

Head

Add straight lines for the shoulders and hips.

Body

Hips

Add the arms and legs with dots to show the joints.

Sketch in simple shapes for the hands and feet.

Add ears and facial details.

Draw in ovals for the knees.

Draw in the shape of the musket.

Add shape to the feet.

Draw in the shape of the hat and clothing.

Sketch in the beard, moustache and hair.

Sketch in the sword and pistols.

Finish the beard and add shading.

Add details to the musket.

Add the shape of the shoes.

Shade all areas where light wouldn't reach.

Add detail to his weapons.

Finish off all the details of the clothing. Add ragged edges and tears.

Add buckles to his shoes and complete all details.

Remember to remove any unwanted construction lines.

Pirate Flags

Hoist the Jolly Roger! The skull and crossbones flag struck terror into all seafarers. Each pirate captain had his own version of the Jolly Roger to identify his ship.

Draw in an arm and hand shape.

Thomas Tew's flag

Now add the fingers clutching a curved cutlass.

Shade in the background.

Henry Avery's flag

Draw the side view of a skull. Add crossbones.

Stede Bonnet's flag

Draw in a pirate and a skeleton.

Bartholomew Roberts's flag

16

Shade in the backgrounds.

Calico Jack Rackham's flag

Sketch in a billowing flag.
Draw in a skull (front view)
and then two crossed swords.

Shade in the background.

Now practice drawing
the same design but on
different flag shapes.

Negative space
Look at the shapes left
between the lines of your
drawing. This can help you
spot mistakes.

Remember to lose sections of the image
where the fabric turns or drapes.

Pirate trio

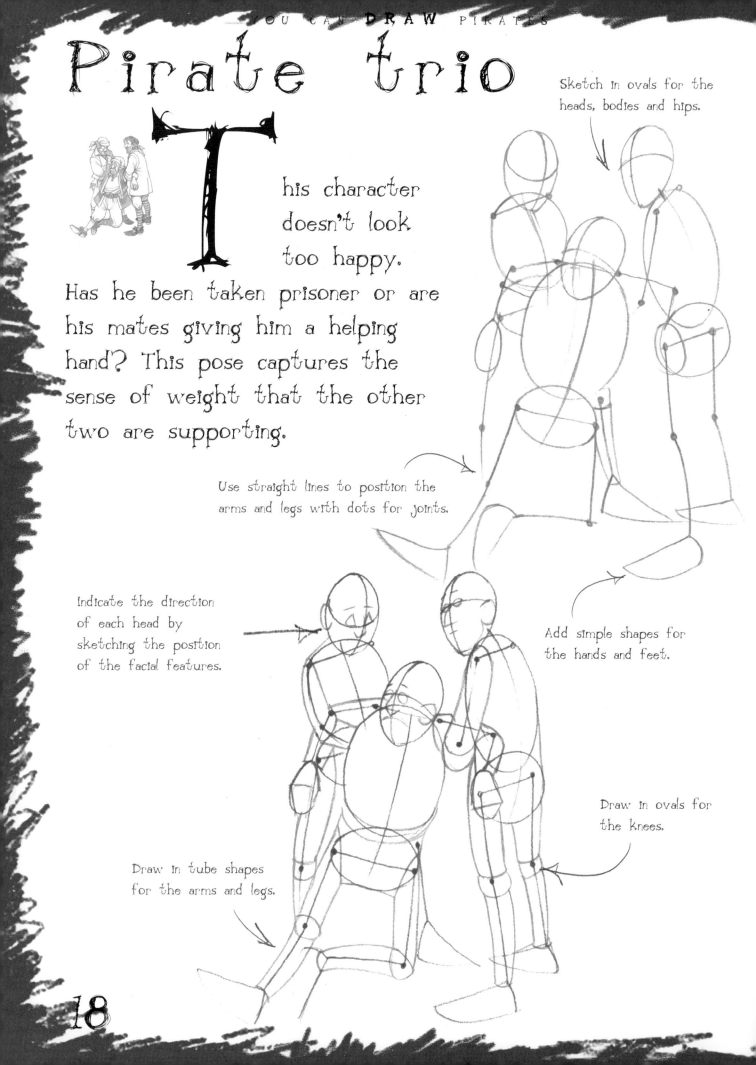

This character doesn't look too happy. Has he been taken prisoner or are his mates giving him a helping hand? This pose captures the sense of weight that the other two are supporting.

Sketch in ovals for the heads, bodies and hips.

Use straight lines to position the arms and legs with dots for joints.

Indicate the direction of each head by sketching the position of the facial features.

Add simple shapes for the hands and feet.

Draw in ovals for the knees.

Draw in tube shapes for the arms and legs.

18

Sketch in the
pirates' headwear.

Draw in the ears and facial features.

Start to draw in the
main shapes of the
clothing and shoes.

Finish off all details to
the clothes and heads.

Add detail to
areas of the
costume, such as
stripy socks.

The sagging tunic adds weight
to the body.

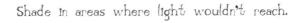

Shade in areas where light wouldn't reach.

19

Buccaneer

Armed to the teeth, this cut-throat pirate is ready to attack. This pose captures a sense of action and excitement.

Sketch in ovals for the head, body and hips. Add straight lines for the shoulders and hips.

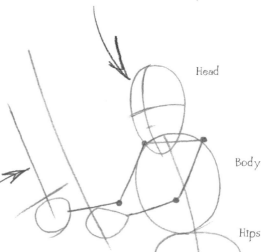

Head

Body

Hips

Add lines for a cutlass in one hand and a dagger in the other.

Add shapes for hands and feet.

Draw in straight lines for the arms and legs.

Draw the hat in around the head.

Use curved lines to add shape to the blades. Draw in handles.

Add the ears and position the facial features.

Using the construction lines as a guide, start drawing in the main shapes of the body.

Sketch in tube shapes for the arms and legs with dots for joints.

Add more shape to the feet.

Add detail to the structure of the hat.

Draw in hair using flowing lines.

Draw in the eyes, nose, ears and mouth.

Add the fingers and thumbs.

Use curved, sweeping lines to draw in the swirl of the topcoat to show movement.

Draw in cuffs on sleeves.

Add large cuffs to the top of the boots.

Add shading to the hat and belt.

Complete the details of the cutlass and dagger.

Add pockets, buttonholes, buttons and patterned cuffs.

Shade all the areas where light wouldn't reach.

Add buckles to the boots.

21

Pirate ships

Pirate ships were generally small, fast ships like sloops that were easy to manoeuvre. Large merchant ships tended to be heavier and slower so they were easy targets for pirates to attack.

Add three lines for the masts.

Draw a long box—like shape on two levels for the ship's hull.

See pages 6–7 to put perspective into use.

Using a high vanishing point, draw in the sails.

Draw in the bowsprit.

Draw in the different deck levels.

Start sketching in the
ship's details now.

Composition

By framing your drawing
with a square or a
rectangle you can make it
look completely different.

Draw a centre line
through the sails.

Draw in straight lines
for the rigging.

Add a flag at the rear.

Add lines along the shape of
the hull to define it.

Add detail to the sails.

Finish off the detail on the
rigging and add masts and rails.

Draw a skull and
crossbones on the flag.

Draw in the decking.

Add cannon ports.

23

Pirate with parrot

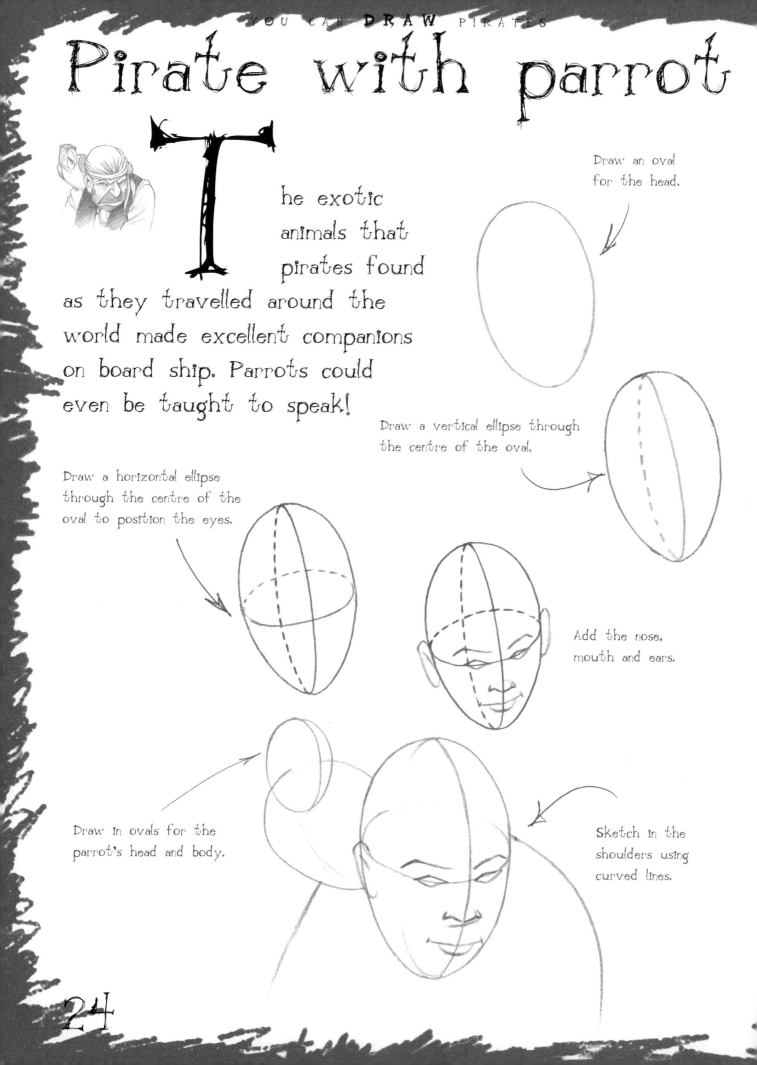

The exotic animals that pirates found as they travelled around the world made excellent companions on board ship. Parrots could even be taught to speak!

Draw an oval for the head.

Draw a vertical ellipse through the centre of the oval.

Draw a horizontal ellipse through the centre of the oval to position the eyes.

Add the nose, mouth and ears.

Draw in ovals for the parrot's head and body.

Sketch in the shoulders using curved lines.

Sketch in the parrot's eyes, beak and wings.

Add detail to the pirate's facial expression.

Draw in more shape to the parrot's head.

Add eyes and markings.

Draw in the bandana.

Finish off facial details.

Sketch in the pirate's clothing.

Use small, broken lines to create feathers.

Add tone with shading.

Shade in any areas where light wouldn't reach.

25

Pirates in action

Pirates relied on speed and terror to attack their victim's ship. Once on board they fought with great fury. This action pose captures the cut and thrust of the attack.

Draw ovals for the head, body and hips of both figures.

Sketch in the straight lines for the arms and legs with dots for joints.

Sketch straight lines for the weapons.

Add simple shapes for the hands and feet.

Note the angle of the feet.

Position the eyes, nose and ears.

Using the construction lines as a guide, draw in the main shapes of the bodies.

Draw in the tube shapes for the arms and legs.

Add fingers and thumbs to the hands.

Add details to the weapons.

Draw in the hat shapes curving around the head.

Sketch large cuffs on the coat.

Add tall over-the-knee boots.

Draw in boots with a fold over the top.

Add detail to the faces and hair.

Draw in all the finishing details to the clothing and boots.

Finish off the daggers and swords.

Add detail to the faces and hair.

Add shading to the areas that light wouldn't reach.

Add buckles.

Remove any unwanted construction lines.

Treasure maps

In pirate stories, 'X' marks the spot where the treasure is buried. In real life, the maps were the real treasure. Knowledge of an area meant the pirates could take their prey by surprise and then quickly disappear again.

Draw a rectangle.

Add a small circle with a vertical and horizontal line through it.

Sketch in three small circles and a cross.

Start sketching in land shapes and islands.

Draw borders inside the rectangle.

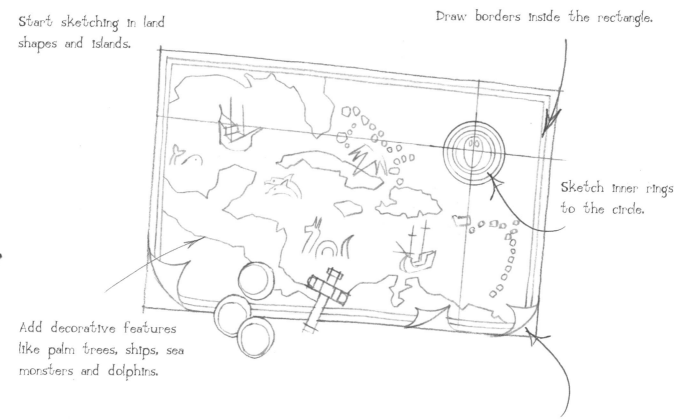

Sketch inner rings to the circle.

Add decorative features like palm trees, ships, sea monsters and dolphins.

Add curled up corners and tears.

28

Draw in more detail on the ships and monsters.

Add more rips and tears. Sketch a pattern in the border.

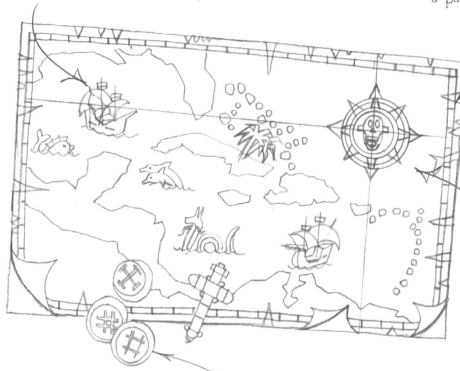

Add a skull and points to the compass.

Add more detail to the cross and the 'pieces of eight.'

Add mid tones and dark tones alternately to the border.

Add tone by shading all the land masses.

Complete all the details on the small drawings.

29

Pirate in the rigging

All hands on deck! To your swords and pistols — battle stations! As the cannons roar, this pirate has scrambled up the rigging to assess the attack. This figure is poised, ready for action.

Sketch in ovals for the head, body and hips.

Draw in straight lines for the rigging.

Add a line for the cutlass.

Head

Body

Hips

Add the hat shape and position the eyes, ear, nose and mouth.

Draw in the curved lines of the cutlass.

Draw in the hand shapes clutching the rigging and the sword.

Use straight lines to position the arms and the legs with dots for the joints.

Using construction lines as a guide, draw in the main shapes of the body.

Sketch in circles and loops for the cross ropes.

Draw in tube shapes for the arms and legs. Add ovals for the knees.

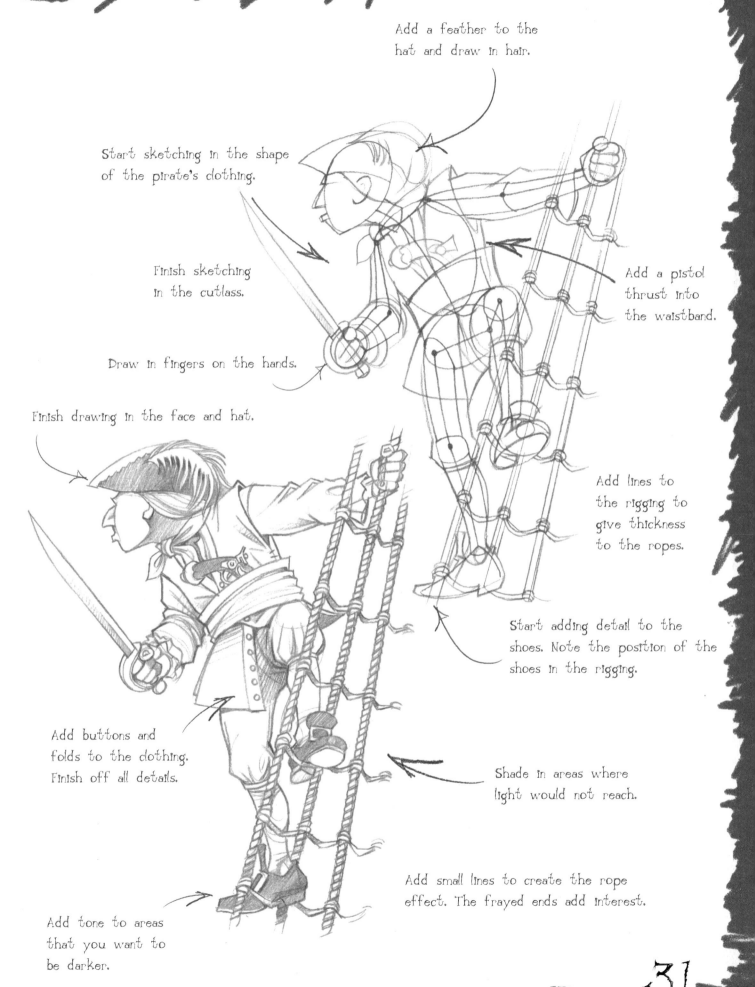

Add a feather to the hat and draw in hair.

Start sketching in the shape of the pirate's clothing.

Finish sketching in the cutlass.

Draw in fingers on the hands.

Add a pistol thrust into the waistband.

Finish drawing in the face and hat.

Add lines to the rigging to give thickness to the ropes.

Start adding detail to the shoes. Note the position of the shoes in the rigging.

Add buttons and folds to the clothing. Finish off all details.

Shade in areas where light would not reach.

Add small lines to create the rope effect. The frayed ends add interest.

Add tone to areas that you want to be darker.

31

Glossary

Bowsprit A pole which extends forward from the front of a ship.

Composition The arrangement of the parts of a picture on the drawing paper.

Construction lines Guidelines used in the early stages of a drawing. They are usually erased later.

Cutlass A curved sword favoured by pirates.

Light source The direction from which the light seems to come in a drawing.

Negative space The space between the parts of a drawing.

Perspective A method of drawing in which near objects are shown larger than faraway objects to give an impression of depth.

Pose The position assumed by a figure.

Proportion The correct relationship of scale between each part of the drawing.

Rigging The ropes which hold a ship's sail up.

Silhouette A drawing that shows only a flat dark shape, like a shadow.

Vanishing point The place in a perspective drawing where parallel lines appear to meet.

Index